GEORGE BENJAMIN

THREE INVENTIONS

FOR CHAMBER
ORCHESTRA

(1993–95)

FABER *ff* MUSIC

PROGRAMME NOTE

Commissioned by Betty Freeman for the 75th Salzburg Festival, this work is scored for an ensemble of 24 players: 7 wind, 4 brass, harp, piano, 2 percussionists and 9 strings. The discrepancy in length and character of the three movements is intentional – two relatively short and light movements preceding a much longer and darker conclusion.

In the first Invention, mainly serene and luminous in atmosphere, a brief introduction leads to a sustained flugel-horn solo whose melodic curves create constantly transforming harmonic implications.

The second Invention is fast, loud and rhythmic. A virtuoso cor anglais solo announces what appears to be a conventional triple metre; however, within a very brief time all manner of irregular figuration and unexpected tempo juxtapositions contort this metre beyond recognition. Halfway through the texture launches into an energetic *tutti*; only at the very end is metrical regularity reinstated by an acrobatic clarinet solo.

The final Invention mirrors the first in technical conception, but the tone is radically different. Antiphonal tuned gongs and bass drums surround a network of materials which weave through the whole ensemble: slow bass octaves, floating consonant harmonies, rushing filigree scales … As these materials rotate across the structure in ever-changing combinations they encounter a variety of foreground melodic solos: initially a serpentine contrabassoon, later a menacing euphonium and more florid violins and violas. As the movement progresses, harmony and rhythm mutate into constantly new territory, but the heavy, bass-dominated pulse which underpins the texture remains remorselessly regular until the very end.

GB

Any pause between the first and second Inventions should be
as brief as possible; there should be a much longer break
between the second and third Inventions.

THREE INVENTIONS
for Chamber Orchestra

I

in memory of Olivier Messiaen

George Benjamin

4

[Note for the conductor: between bars 13-24 all dynamics are relative;
the whole passage must be played *sotto voce*, with the utmost delicacy]

*A tenor trombone straight mute is recommended for the Flugelhorn; despite the mute the Flugel solo must dominate the texture at all times
**Until the end of bar 69 *all* unaccented semiquavers as soft as possible

12

18

II

*Violins: if fingering of any chord is impossible, omit the lowest note
**Violas: if fingering of any chord is impossible, omit the highest note

*Vc. ossia: omit open D

III

for Alexander Goehr

† molto pesante, tenuto, senza dim.: sempre sim.

† See note, p.37

*Strings, bars 16-53: stressed notes (♪) to be played **pp**, slightly stretched in length (even *poco vibrato*); all other
fast notes to be played **pppp** *poss.*, and slightly rushed to compensate for the stretched notes

*See note, p.39

† See note, p.37
* See note, p.39

42

† See note, p.37

† See note, p.37

44

*See note, p.39

49

52

*pp sub. : full-length, light bows on each note

*Accented figuration: each accent clear and hard; all
notes *sempre ben in tempo* (unlike earlier *tenuto* notes).

*See note, p.55

* Harp, bars 109-118: pull the string as hard as possible to produce a harsh, twanging sound